MEL BAY PRESENTS

SOLOS FOR GUITAR

Frederic Hand

Online Audio

To Access the Online Audio Go To:
www.melbay.com/98190BCDEB

ONLINE AUDIO

1	Elegy for a King [3:01]	7	About Time [3:55]
2	A Dance for John Dowland [1:40]	8	A Celtic Tale [2:10]
3	Desert Sketch [1:30]	9	Lesley's Song [3:01]
4	Simple Gifts [3:12]	10	Heart's Song [5:29]
5	Missing Her [4:30]	11	For Lenny [3:40]
6	A Waltz for Maurice [4:33]		

Cover art courtesy of David Hornung

Visit us on the Web at www.melbay.com — E-mail us at email@melbay.com

Table of Contents

PREFACE

The compositions in this collection are drawn from different periods in my life and have all been either revised, adapted or written for this publication. The earliest works, *Elegy for a King* and *A Dance for John Dowland* were composed when I was in college. More recently composed pieces are *For Lenny, About Time* and *Desert Sketch. Heart's Song* and *Missing Her* were originally composed for various small ensembles that featured the guitar. Those works lent themselves to a solo adaptation. It is my intention that all of the music in this collection be appropriate for the concert stage, but also, to be accessible to the student guitarist. At first glance, some of the music may appear more difficult than it actually is. This relates to its readability rather than technical difficulty. Over the past few decades, enormous strides have been made regarding the technical proficiency of classical guitarists, but sight reading still poses a considerable challenge for most. The upper positions of the instrument can be especially foreign, even for more experienced players. In order to play the music in this collection, it will be necessary to become familiar with the upper positions of the guitar, as many of the chords are voiced there.

Personally, the attraction of the classical guitar is its warmth of tone and resonance. I'm particularly fond of voicing harmonies tightly, often including the rub of a minor second. This is achieved by combining fretted notes on the upper positions of the finger board, with open strings. While it might take longer at first to figure out what is being called for, most of the harmonies fall quite happily under the fingers. When a difficult technique is required, I've offered easier alternative possibilities for the passage. The fingerings are offered as a guide, and need not be rigidly followed. Most important is the comfort with which the music is played, and the bringing out of its essential qualities. While it is desirable to play the notes as they are written and on the strings that are indicated, it is better to simplify a chord or passage rather than to struggle and sacrifice the flow and spirit of the music.

The accompanying recording of these compositions may contain some minor variations from the printed page. This is due to the fact that try as I may, I'm incapable of playing my own pieces exactly as I have set them down on paper. Where there are discrepancies, feel free to play whichever version you prefer.

PROGRAM NOTES

Elegy For a King - In 1968 America was suffering through a period of political upheaval. The Vietnam War was raging, the country was divided, and the Civil Rights Movement continued to challenge the moral conscience of the country. *Elegy for a King* was written in memory of Dr. Martin Luther King Jr., in the wake of the sudden loss of a great universal spirit.

A Dance for John Dowland - As one of the greatest composer's of the Elizabethan era, John Dowland's music has, for me, stood out as among the finest examples of pre-Bach contrapuntal writing. Having been introduced to Dowland's music as a teenager through the great recordings of Julian Bream, his lute songs, consort arrangements, and solo lute literature have always been personal favorites of mine. Many of his works have dedications not only to the people influential in his life, such as his employer, Queen Elizabeth, but to a wide variety of characters about whom little is known. Having played a great deal of his music on both the guitar and lute, as a nineteen year old, I was inspired to write a piece for him.

Desert Sketch - After a week of camping in the canyon lands of southern Utah, the indescribable beauty of the high desert remained clear in my mind's eye. Long after the trip, as I would recall my experiences of the vistas, wild life, and sudden and unpredictable changes in atmosphere and weather, musical impulses would arise. They were set down here in the form of a short sketch.

3

Simple Gifts - This arrangement for guitar of a famous Shaker Song is my homage to Aaron Copland. His masterful setting of this tune in his ballet, *Appalachian Spring*, was my inspiration.

Missing Her - When I was a student at the Mannes College of Music, it was an oddity to find musicians accomplished in both classical music and jazz improvisation. Now it is much more common for young musicians to be well versed in both traditions. Musical boundaries are routinely being crossed and the result is a lot of new and exciting music. My own training was almost exclusively as a classical guitarist, but as a teenager I fell in love with the sounds of Miles Davis, Bill Evans, John Coltrane, and many other modern jazz artists. *Missing Her* was one my first attempts to include an improvisatory section in the midst of a fully composed piece. Initially, I thought of writing out an improvisation for this edition, as not all guitarists possess improvisational skills. I tried, but as soon as something was set down on paper, it became frozen and sounded composed. In addition to a prerequisite knowledge of harmony, intervals and modes, improvisation requires a trust that, in the moment, something worthwhile will come out of one's instrument. For me, improvisation is one of the great joys music has to offer. So for those of you who are adventurous and so inclined, here is *Missing Her*.

A Waltz for Maurice - One of the ways in which I supported myself for many years was as a writer of music for television. One day I got a call from a music producer asking me to write a theme for a new character on a show, a young ballet dancer. I pictured the dancer doing her warm up exercises. What quickly came to mind was a waltz theme, "classical" in nature. It quickly developed into more of an impressionistic style and soon I was exploring the harmonic language of one of my favorite composers, Maurice Ravel. Sometimes it's possible to look back at a piece and know with absolute certainty what the musical inspiration for it was. In this case it was from the middle movement of Ravel's *Piano Concerto in G major*, one of the most strikingly beautiful themes ever written.

About Time is a study in changing time meters. Many of these meters, such as 7/8, 5/8 or unusual groupings of 9/8, are common to musicians from the Middle East and the Mediterranean countries, but less common for the Western musician. By now though, they have found their way into the mainstream of contemporary musical language, in classical, jazz and world music. I have written an optional improvisatory section for those who are interested in exploring that aspect of music making.

A Celtic Tale - Ever since I was a little boy I have been drawn to the folk music of the British Isles. To me this music possesses a haunting beauty that is both powerful and elegant in its simplicity. In the world of classical music, two of my favorite English composers, Ralph Vaughn Williams and Benjamin Britten, have frequently written works that owe their inspiration to the vast number of country dances and folk songs of England, Scotland and Ireland. *A Celtic Tale* was inspired by a film I'd seen about a theatrical company touring the small villages throughout Ireland. More than the story itself, it was the lushness and deep green of the Irish countryside that moved me to write this piece.

Lesley's Song. I composed this piece for my wife and my best friend, Lesley.

Heart's Song is the name of a recording of original compositions which feature the guitar with different instrumental combinations. It is also the name of the title piece, the original instrumentation being for guitar, cello and synthesizer. I hear in it three distinct musical influences. The opening and closing sections are Spanish-Romantic in nature and somewhat reminiscent of the music of Joaquin Rodrigo. The middle section was originally intended to be a separate piece, to be entitled *Intermezzo*. It reminded me in temperament of the passionate intermezzi for piano of Johannes Brahms. Harmonically, the last section reveals my love and attraction to the music of contemporary Brazil. The outer sections of *Heart's Song* utilize a right hand technique that is a cross between an arpeggio and a tremolo and may feel awkward at first. This is a technique for the more advanced guitarist, and one that is worth developing because it has other useful applications, such as for cross-string trills. For those who would prefer a simpler but still effective alternative arpeggio is offered.

For Lenny - After viewing a documentary film on the life of Leonard Bernstein, I was inspired to write this short piece in his memory. His music has always spoken to my deepest emotions, and I remain touched by his genius, musical conviction, and above all, tremendous heart.

BIOGRAPHY

Frederic Hand was born in Brooklyn, New York in 1947. He attended New York's High School of Music and Art and is a graduate of the Mannes College of Music. In 1972 he received a Fulbright Scholarship to study in England with Julian Bream. His concert career, both as a soloist and with his ensemble Jazzantiqua, have met with the highest critical acclaim and include performances throughout North and South America, Europe and Scandinavia. As a guest artist, Frederic Hand has performed with the New York Philharmonic, Mostly Mozart Orchestra, Music from Marlboro, Orchestra of St. Luke's and the Waverly Consort. In 1986 he was appointed guitarist and lutenist with the Metropolitan Opera and has accompanied among others, Luciano Pavarotti and Placido Domingo. In addition to recordings for Sony, RCA, Music Masters and the Musical Heritage Society, he has composed music for film and television for which he has won an Emmy Award. Frederic Hand serves on the faculty of the Mannes College of Music in New York City and is the director of the guitar program at Purchase College, State University of New York. He lives in upstate New York with his wife, Lesley.

Credits:
Cover art: David Hornung
CD produced by Frederic Hand
CD engineered and mastered by Suzanne Kapa and John Yates.
Special thanks to Giacomo LaVita for his invaluable assistance
in the preparation of these manuscripts.

In Memory of Martin Luther King Jr.

Elegy for a King

Frederic Hand

6

This page has been left blank to avoid awkward page turns

A Dance for John Dowland

Frederic Hand

10

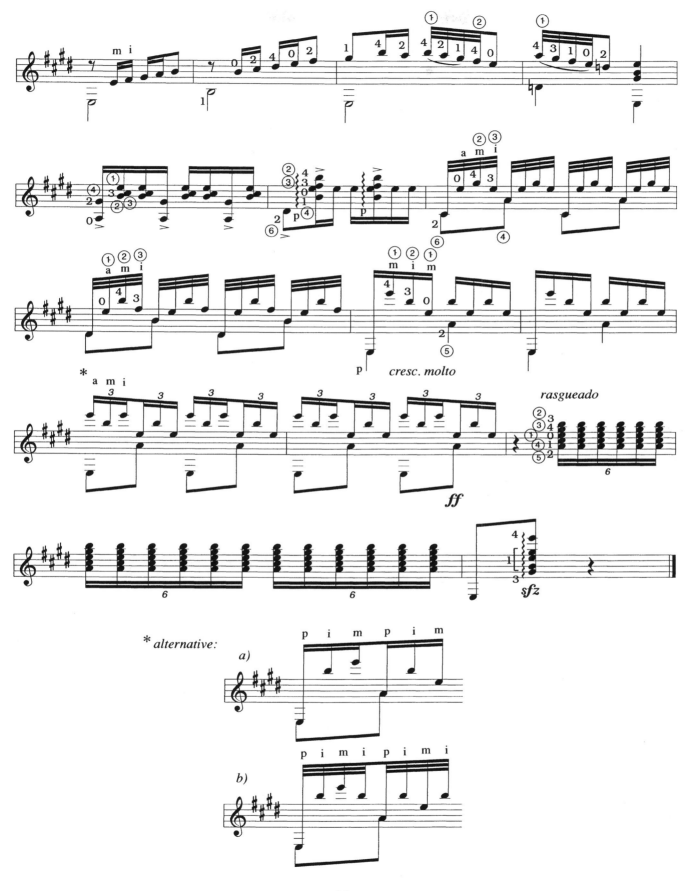

Desert Sketch

Frederic Hand

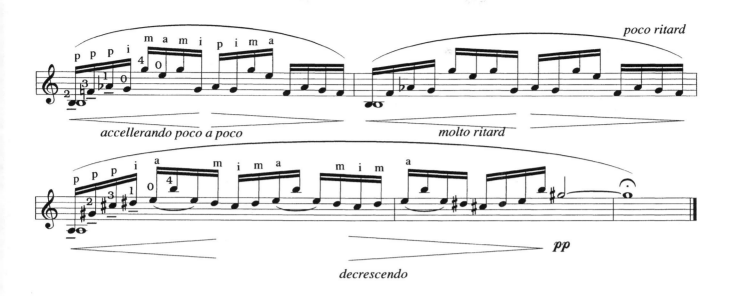

This page has been left blank to avoid awkward page turns

Simple Gifts

Traditional Shaker Tune
Arranged by Frederic Hand

15

Tender and expressive
slower

Broadly

16

Missing Her

Frederic Hand

Improvisation
jazz waltz feel

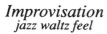

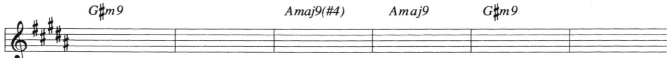

21

tempo of jazz waltz

CVII

CVII

freely

15
Harm. ————
rit. - - - - - - - - -

tamboura (strike strings
with back of thumb near bridge)

A Waltz for Maurice

Frederic Hand

24

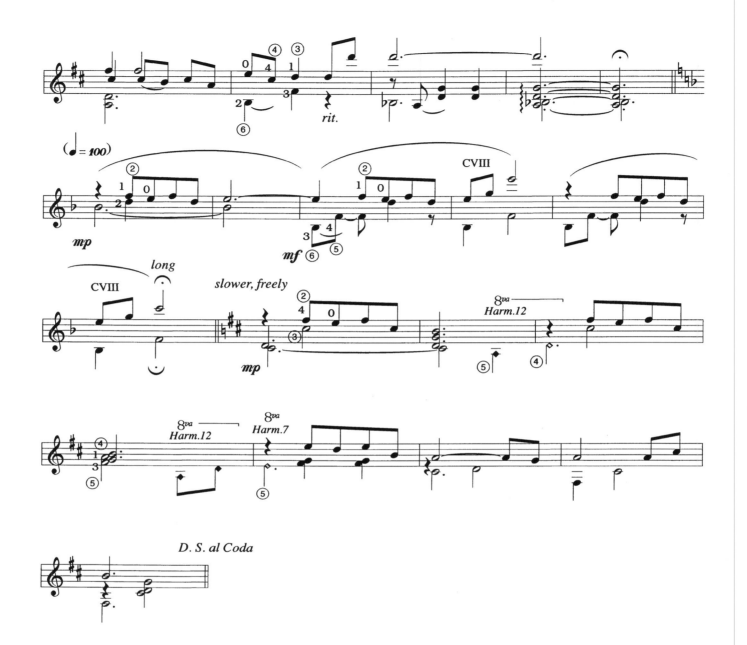

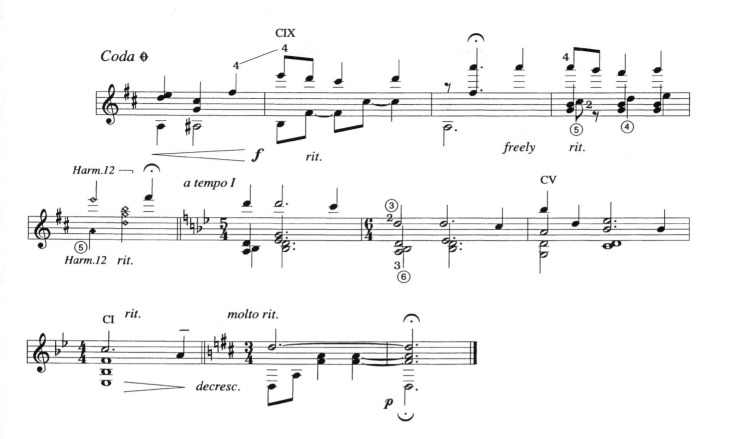

About Time

Allegro

Frederic Hand

29

This is an optional improvisatory section. For those who do not wish to improvise, proceed to the coda. The purpose of this section is to express spontaneity and rhythmic playfulness. The following ideas are presented only as suggestions of possibilities to be improvised upon. Feel free to disregard them altogether or to modify or expand them, as well as to create original material. At the conclusion of this section, proceed to the coda.

repeat several times, fading into inaudibility

A Celtic Tale

Tenderly, poco rubato

Frederic Hand

Lesley's Song

Heart's Song

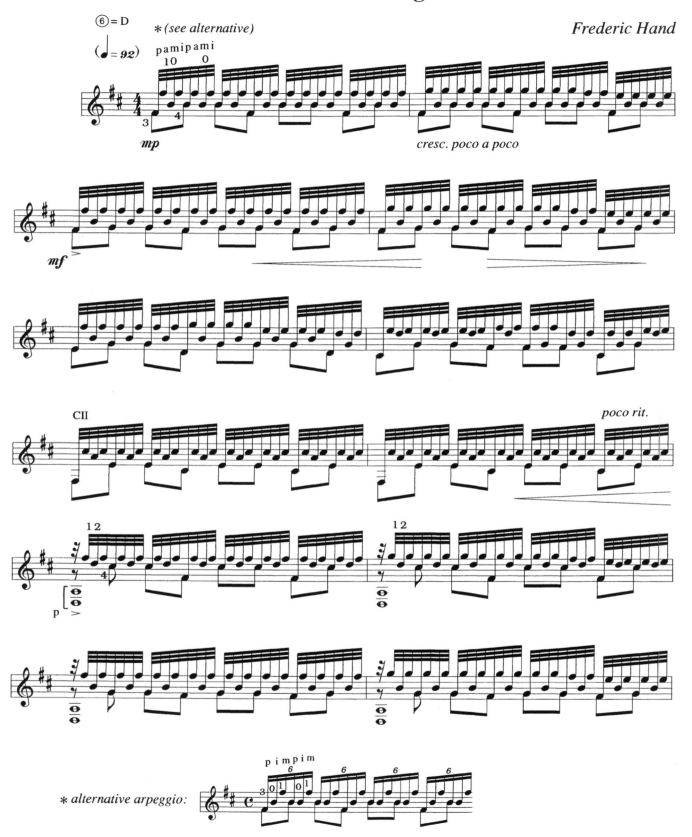

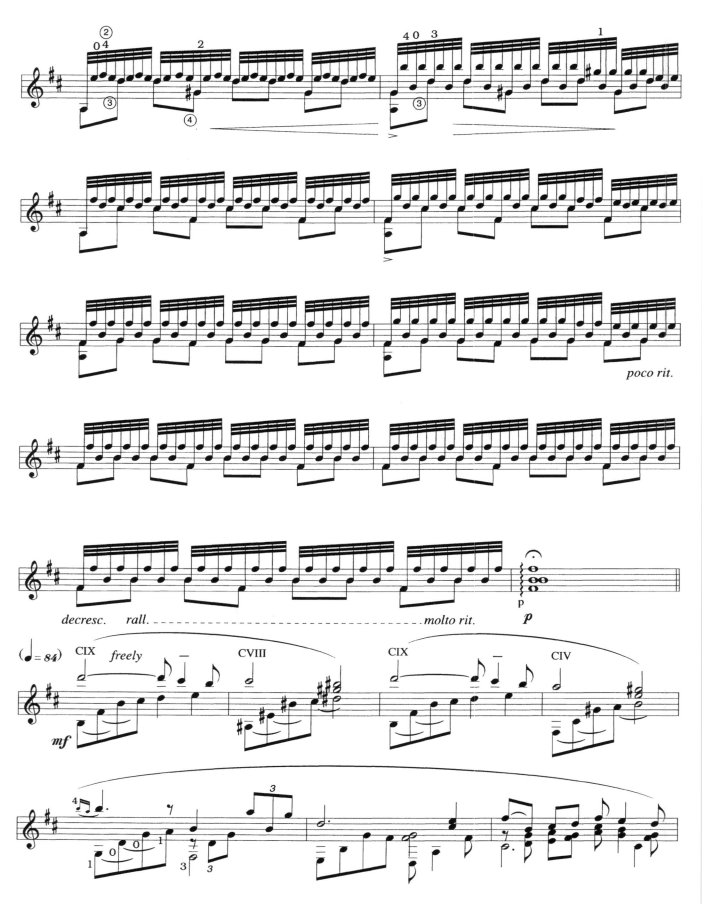

41

*see alternative arpeggio in opening section

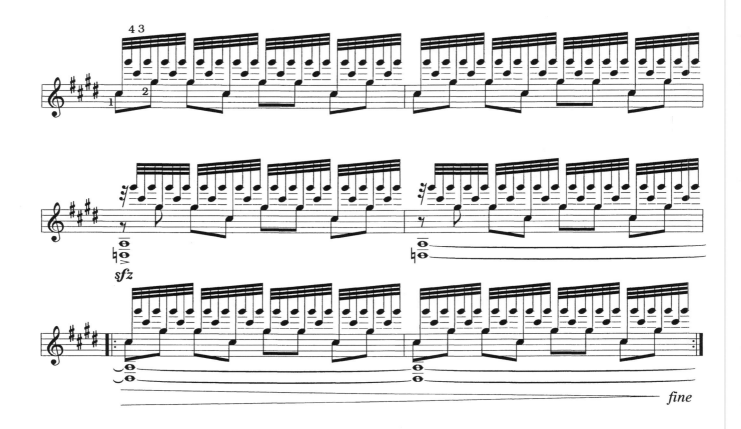

Repeat several times while fading into inaudibility. Do not play the bass notes "D" and "A" while fading.

This page has been left blank to avoid awkward page turns

For Lenny

(to Leonard Bernstein)

Frederic Hand

Tempo 1

mp

mf

f

47

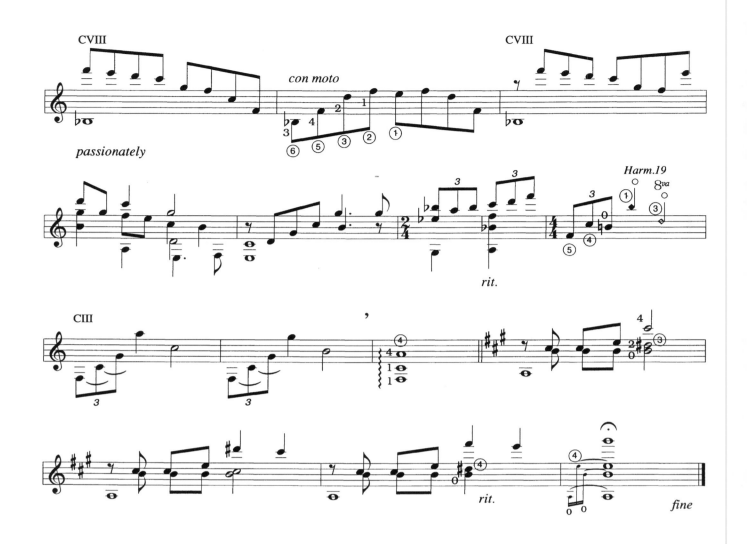